THE MERGE
*A Reemerging of the
Sacred Feminine and Sacred Masculine*

THE MERGE IS BOOK THREE OF THE NEW EDEN SERIES

OTHER BOOKS BY JAMES GALLUZZO

Sacred Feminine *(Book One of the New Eden Series)*
Sacred Masculine *(Book Two of the New Eden Series)*
A Spiritual Handbook: A Resource for Travelers and Guides on the Journey
The Spirituality of Mary Magdalene
Jesus as Liberator and the Gospel Values
Quotes and Reflection Questions for Journaling your Spiritual Journey
Spiritual Writing: Be the Author of Your Own Story
Stop Whining, Choose Life.

THE MERGE
*A Reemerging of the
Sacred Feminine and Sacred Masculine*

JAMES GALLUZZO

Gray Wings Press, LLC
Milwaukie, Oregon
2014

THE MERGE
*A Reemerging of the
Sacred Feminine and Sacred Masculine*

By James Galluzzo

Library of Congress Control Number: 2014945577

Copyright © 2014 James Galluzzo

All rights are reserved under International and Pan-American Copyright Conventions.

No part of this book may be used or reproduced in any manner without permission except in the case of brief quotations in critical articles or reviews.

Requests should be forwarded to diversityasgift@comcast.net

or sent to Gray Wings Press, P.O. Box 593, Clackamas, OR 97015

ISBN 978-0692247198

*Dedicated to
the sacred women and men
who have lit the way for all of us.*

THE MERGE
*A Reemerging of the
Sacred Feminine and Sacred Masculine*

Six Paintings

This final installment of six new paintings for the New Eden Series shows the *Sacred Feminine* and the *Sacred Masculine* joined together. I honor our humanity at its fullest, individually and collectively. The art invites a new way of thinking, a new way of living and a new way of loving in the union, actually reunion, of these two images. I believe that, once we make the connection between our Sacred Masculine and Sacred Feminine, we can rediscover our whole self, free of conditioning, and can move toward peace and holiness, toward a world of connectedness and oneness.

By James Galluzzo

"WHEN THE SACRED FEMININE AND SACRED MASCULINE MERGE
WE WILL CREATE A NEW EDEN – WE WILL RECLAIM
THE SACRED FEMININE AND SACRED MASCULINE AS ONE."

JAMES GALUZZO

INTRODUCTION

This book is the third and final work in the New Eden series. First was the Sacred Feminine that honored the history of the feminine. The second book was the Sacred Masculine that honored the four traditional archetypes plus the two new ones: the Father and the Grounded One.

Six themes are represented by the paintings described in this third book and address the reemerging of the Sacred Feminine and Sacred Masculine – the new Eden, pain and possibility, the sacred call, the new trinity, the history and the cosmic union. As in the prior works, each chapter discusses one painting and its wording and expands the concept with related poems, reflections, quotations and prayers that speak to the painting and explain its symbology.

A BRIEF HISTORY OF THE SACRED FEMININE AND SACRED MASCULINE

We are born whole and fully human with our Sacred Masculine and Sacred Feminine connected and intact within us and with others. This is our natural state of being and potential whether we are two weeks old, twenty years old or a hundred and two years old. As we grow, we learn more; we have a history and our story continues; it builds from our experiences and we grow in wisdom and knowledge. But from birth, we are human. So the merge of the Sacred Masculine and Sacred Feminine is not a new concept. It is a remembrance of who we are in our core essence.

The need to jump start this reconnection manifests when, along the way, we get messages that tell us we are less than human; we act out differently to conform to those messages and stray from our humanity. Some examples are when we are ridiculed for crying, for being weak, for being creative, for being tough, and for being different. These are social conditions based on misunderstanding, prejudice, racism, homophobia, sexism, adultism and classism, any abusive behavior that oppresses people in any way. In response, we adopt the illusion that we are not enough, we are not perfect, we are less than, we are unworthy. We forget that our humanness is universal, permanent, whole and complete, unconditional, limitless and unique. We cover up falsely because we feel our humanity is lost and wish to avoid the train wreck of old hurts and pains and misinformation.

To rediscover our truth is to acknowledge every feeling and to face each feeling (don't deny it; it is a real feeling whether based on reality or not). Healing comes from knowing what we are feeling, embracing the feeling and then discharging it by talking about it, writing about it, crying it out or any other form of discharge. Ask for help. We can heal the old hurts and false messages by stepping out of isolation or resentment or guilt or fear and engaging in spiritual practices, or working with a spiritual director or counselor.

Our ancestors have showed us the way of living fully and being authentic in how they followed their hearts. Some of those stories are reflected in the paintings in this book and referenced especially in Chapter 5. Embracing the Sacred Feminine and Sacred Masculine is reclaiming our full self to live our life fully. Every man, woman and child is fully human and is inherently connected to themselves, others, the world, the universe and the sacred.

THE MERGE OF THE SACRED MASCULINE AND SACRED FEMININE

As we reemerge

    All that disconnects us

    Will become one

We will claim power with, instead of power over

We will be gentle and kind, instead of judging others

We will be affirming of all people, instead of being prejudicial

We will be filled with abundance and goodness, instead of greed

We will be good stewards of creation

We will care for those who are struggling

We will honor the old and the young

We will treat all with dignity

And then women and men will be one

And we will create a new garden

A new paradise

We shall reclaim Eden once again

And then the greed of some will give way to the needs of many.

James Galluzzo inspired by Judy Chicago

Chapter One: The Merge Creates a New Eden..... 1

Chapter Two: Pain and Possibilities... 7

Chapter Three: Sacred is the Call........ 13

Chapter Four: The New Trinity............ 19

Chapter Five: The History of the Union.................... 25

Chapter Six: The Cosmic Union.......... 31

Chapter One

THE MERGE CREATES A NEW EDEN

THE MERGE CREATES A NEW EDEN

(*as seen on painting*)

Women and men together

Sacred Masculine merges with Sacred Feminine

Merge within each person

Men and women are gentle

Woman and men are strong

Together

A new Eden

One

As one we create a garden

We garden together

Paradise

Working together, men and women, side by side, this is what we have been waiting for, working for, dreaming of, and creating together. From this action we honor our ancestors, the holy women and men, who courageously fought for justice, equality and the sacred union, and we reclaim our natural birthright to be inherently human and inherently connected. When women and men work together they are planting a new garden while being both gentle and strong, powerful and thoughtful, emotional and clear thinking, prophetic and mystical, and loving and caring.

This painting represents the theme that when the Sacred Masculine and Sacred Feminine merge, a new garden and a new Eden are created, a new garden where everyone and every creature are treated with respect and dignity.

Prayers & Poems to:
The Merge Creates a New Eden

THE MERGE

May the merge of the Sacred Feminine and Sacred Masculine within you, bless you, nurture you and create new life within you.
James Galluzzo

THE BELOVED

The Sacred Masculine and Sacred Feminine is the union of the beloved, the desire for equality. This is our journey to reclaim our connectedness, to be one with, to be fully human, to be all that we are called to be.
James Galluzzo

CREATION OF GOD

While I know myself as a creation of God, I am also obligated to realize and remember that everyone else and everything else are also God's creation.
Maya Angelou

LOOKING FOR THE BOY AND GIRL IN EACH OF US

Has anyone seen the boy who used to come here?
Round-faced troublemaker, quick to find a joke,
Slow to be serious, red shirt, perfect coordination, sly, strong, muscled
With things always in his pocket:
Reed flute, worn pick, polished and ready for this Talent.
You know that one.
Have you heard stories about him?
Pharaoh and the whole Egyptian world collapsed for such a Joseph.
I'd gladly spend years getting word of him, even third or fourth hand.
Rumi

HAS ANYONE SEEN THE GIRL WHO USED TO COME HERE?

Bright smiling rabble rouser, quick to solve a riddle
Always climbing trees and scraping her knees
Slow to cry or give up a dare
With things in her pocket:
A sling shot, a top, a reed to blow and a string or match if needed
You know her.
Have you heard stories of her?
I would collapse for such a woman.
I gladly spend years getting word of her, even third or fourth hand.
James Galluzzo

Chapter Two

PAIN AND POSSIBILITIES

PAIN AND POSSIBILITIES
(as seen on painting)

Every woman

Every man

Friends

One

Partners

To lay down

Compassion

Love

Healers

Together

Suffering

Passion

Love to lay down your life for a friend

Life and death together

Together, new life

Hands made for holding

Arms made for support

Love, pain, passion, compassion, care

Blood sweat tears

Heart connection

Pain and possibilities

Nails and hearts

In the process of embracing the Sacred Masculine and Sacred Feminine, there are many struggles and many discoveries. We call these pains and possibilities.

The pain calls us to review our lives – where have we settled for less; where have we let conditioning from culture, religion and society affect our lives; where have we bought into the victim or oppressor roles; where have we colluded with racism, sexism, homophobia or any other forms of oppression; where have we failed to forgive ourselves or others; and where have we isolated or disconnected from ourselves, others, our call or the sacred?

The possibilities call us to dream - to imagine new ways of thinking, feeling deciding and acting; to reconnect to ourselves, to all men, to all women, to the universe, to the sacred; to think and live resiliently; to embrace diversity as a gift and to explain and embrace what it means to be fully human.

Looking at both the pain and possibilities takes courage, support, practice, loving kindness, taking care of ourselves and committing to do nothing that hurts us, nothing that hurts others, to not let others hurt us and to work to end any behavior that mistreats human beings or gets in the way of any person's humanity.

This painting represents the pain and possibilities with the symbols of nails and hearts. It captures the struggles and the hopes; the blood, sweat and tears; the joys and sorrows; the successes and mistakes; forgiveness and reconciliation; and the need to have support along the journey.

Prayers & Poems to:
Pain and Possibilities

LOVE AND FEAR

There is no fear in love; but perfect love casts out fear.
> *1 John 4:18*

ADVICE

Someone dancing inside us learned only a few steps:

The "Do-Your-Work" in 4/4 time,

The "What-Do-You-Expect" waltz

He hasn't noticed yet the woman standing away from the lamp;

The one with black eyes who knows the rhumba,

And strange steps on jumpy rhythms from the mountains in Bulgaria.

If they dance together,

Something unexpected will happen.

If they don't, the next world will be a lot like this one.
> *Bill Holm*

MISUNDERSTOOD BOYS

But we enjoyed playing games and
> were punished for them by men who played games themselves.

However, grown-up games are known as "business."

And even though boys' games are much the same,

they are punished for them by their elders.

No one pities either the boys or the men, though surely we deserved pity.
> *St. Augustine*

UNHAPPY AND HAPPY

Men and women are infinitely ingenious in their ability to find ways of being unhappy together.
Lawrence Kubie

Women and men are inherently capable in their ability to finds ways of being happy together.
James Galluzzo

STRONG CHILDREN

It is easier to build strong children than to repair broken men.
Frederick Douglass

PAIN AND POSSIBILITIES

Pain offers the possibility of gifts, gifts of being listened to, cared for, thought well of, loved, fed and generally being taken care of. The possibilities are endless.

Pain may require re-visioning life and making choices. The possibilities are endless. Pain makes us vulnerable, open to others, open to relinquishing control and exploring what is really important.

Pain and possibility equal life.
Annie Doyle

Chapter Three

SACRED IS THE CALL

SACRED IS THE CALL
(as seen on painting)

Sacred is the Call

Sacred Masculine
Sacred Feminine as One

Sacred is our call

Sister star

Brother star

One star

Sister sun

One sun brother sun

One

We shall all be well and be one

Supporters

Friends

Travelers

Seekers

Dreamers

Teachers

Lovers

Helpers

Sister moon

Brother moon

Sacred is our call. It is not meant for a few or many, but for all people. The sacred call is to be one and to come together in wholeness. Spirituality is inherent in our nature, as is connection, interdependence and love. The inherent human qualities call us to be the whole, to be at one with ourselves, others, our work in the world, the universe and whatever is holy in our lives. This merger of wholeness is the joining of the Sacred Feminine and Sacred Masculine together in being our authentic and complete self. The merge means not settling for less through echoing scarcity, but living in abundance and settling for nothing less than everything.

This painting represents the universal and sacred call to be fully human. The merge of the Sacred Feminine and Sacred Masculine is an infinite connection creating the journey of the yin and yang, the sun and the moon, the male and female, and the body and soul. Its colors are red, orange and yellow and are filled with light, life and passion. The merge of the primary colors of red and yellow make orange. The whole picture gives out radiance and light.

Prayers & Poems to:
Sacred is the Call

THE CALL

Two eyes to look at the Divine
Two ears to hear the call;
Two feet to walk the way;
Two hands to hold one another,
And one heart to love all.
    Wales Traditional Prayer

WISDOM

Wisdom is a paradox, which never juxtaposes opposites into "either-or" pairs but gathers them onto "both-and" relationships.
    Ann Ulanow

When I sense the holiness of my own body, I begin to sense the call of the holiness of every other body.
    James Nelson

SACRED COMMUNITY

We will go into the future as a single, sacred community of men and women, or we will all perish in the desert.
    Thomas Berry

GOD'S HUG

You are encircled by the arms of the mystery of God.
    Hildegard of Bingen

HE DESIRED ME

He desired me so I came close.
He sang again, a song even sweeter,
And when I tried to shame myself once more from divine presence
God showed me compassion and spoke a divine truth,
I made you, dear, and all I make is perfect.
Please come close, for I desire you.
    St. Teresa of Avila

HUSH

Love set the Universe in motion, set it alive.
Out of Tiamat* you came –
>Out of its destruction
>You were born

Hush. Can you hear your heart speaking to you?
Hush, yet again. Be still.
>Your heart is – and always has been – speaking great things to you.
>Whispering or crying out mysteries that are meant only for you to hear.

Do you hear them?
Love calls you to live fully, to embrace the treasures within –
>The gold and silver of your life.

You are here – wealthy with gifts beyond measure.
How will you live "your one wild and precious life"?**
Love calls, shouts, clamors for your attention, seeking your awakening.
Hush.
There is a rustle in your heart where your wings begin to flutter.
Your heart is stirring.
You hear the sacred Voice.
The Holy is moving within you.
It is your Holy calling to step forward, rich in confidence that Love steadies you in your onward movement.
You take the step: it is the only thing you can do to satisfy your heart's passion.
Your heart desires to fulfill all that it was created to be.
Follow the fire in your heart:
>Warm the world with its heat---
>Light the darkness with its glowing flames and embers---
>Change the world with its powerful energy.

This, this is your call---
Your Sacred call.
>*Susan Hammond*

* *Tiamat: A star that exploded in a supernova that dispersed new elemental power into the Universe.*

** *The Summer Day by Mary Oliver*

Chapter Four

THE NEW TRINITY

THE NEW TRINITY

(as seen on painting)

Sun and moon

Sun garden

United as one

Universal

Unity

Unity in Diversity as Gift,
inherent connection,
embracing peace

Universal peace

World peace

Inner peace

One

Un

'Evag

Tnk

--

Oanh

Ein

One

Uno

Moja

'Biri

The New Trinity represents the Native American idea of joining the feminine and masculine. When they are joined, we experience a serenity that leads to peace. The joining of the Sacred Masculine and Sacred Feminine create a spirit of peace. This peace includes inner peace, world peace and universal peace.

The painting represents the masculine and feminine clothed together in the robes of union. The love of the feminine and the masculine create Sophia – the sacred wisdom that represents peace and the merge of the Sacred Masculine and Sacred Feminine. The halos on the masculine and feminine symbolize the radiance within each and the radiance created through the merge. The Native American spirituality, along with the Celtic, earth and creation spiritualties, does not hold to the idea of dualism*; therefore it is much easier for these traditions to honor and respect the sacred union.

This union creates the third image of the Trinity represented by the dove.

*Dualism (from the Latin word duo meaning "two")[1] denotes a state of two parts. The term 'dualism' was originally coined to denote co-eternal binary opposition.

Moral dualism is the belief of the great complement or conflict between the benevolent and the malignant. It simply implies that there are two moral opposites at work, independent of any interpretation of what might be "moral" and independent of how these may be represented. The moral opposites might, for example, exist in a worldview as between good and evil, or bright and dark, or summer and winter.

Alternatively, in ontological dualism, the world is divided into two overarching categories. The opposition and combination of the universe's two basic principles of yin and yang.

In theology, dualism can refer to the relationship between God and creation. The Christian dualism of God and creation exists in some traditions of Christianity. e.g. the Byzantine Christian sect believed that the universe created through evil, exists separately from a moral God. The Indian philosophy also espouses a dualism between God and the universe. Fundamentalists believe that the soul is good and the body is a temptation. from Wikipedia.

Dualism in this book refers to separating into either/or, e.g. male or female, soul or body, heaven or earth, light or dark. Dualism does not only separate, but places one over the other and often makes one less than the other, e.g. light is good, dark is bad, soul is good, body is evil. The Native Americans and Creation spiritualties see light and dark as good, the soul and body as good.

PRAYERS AND POEMS TO:
THE NEW TRINITY

BROTHER AND SISTER

And I know that the spirit of God is the brother of my own,
And that all the men ever born are also my brothers…
Walt Whitman

And I know that the spirit of God is the sister of my own
And that all women ever born are also my sisters…
And I know that the spirit of God
     is the human connection of my own,
And that all humans ever born are also connected to me.
James Galluzzo

ONE IN PEACE

May we truly become one, so that we can be peacemakers within, among and throughout all of creation. May we have inner peace, world peace and universal peace.
Tina Jones

BELOVED

The Sacred Masculine and the Sacred Feminine are each other's beloved. They long to birth peace.
David Gold

DIVINE PARENT

May the holistic reality of the Divine Parent within you bless you, sustain you and create new life within you.

Gard Jamenson

UNION

My beloved grows
Right out of my own heart
How much more union can there be.

Rumi

POWER OF THE CIRCLE

The life of humans is a circle from childhood to childhood
And so it is in everything where power moves.

Black Elk

CONNECTION TO ALL

We all flow from one fountain. All are expressions of one love. God does not appear, and flow out, only from narrow chinks and round bored wells here and there in favored races and places, but God flows in grand undivided currents, shoeless and boundless over creeds and forms and all kinds of cavitations and people and beasts, saturating all and fountainizing all.

John Muir

Chapter Five

THE HISTORY OF THE UNION

THE HISTORY OF THE UNION

(as seen on painting)

History

The Merge of the Sacred Feminine and
Sacred Masculine holds forth love
for all humanity and
deep connection to everyone

The Sacred Feminine and
Sacred Masculine knows no boundaries

The Sacred Feminine and
Sacred Masculine loves every color

Human Functions:
feel, think, act and decide

Human characteristics:
unconditional, whole/complete, universal

Permanent, limitless, unique

The Sacred Feminine and
Sacred Masculine are free of judgment
and fear & full of love

The Sacred Masculine & Sacred Feminine
knows every gender and loves them

Martyrs Cosmas & Damian -
their lives, love & service to all people.
Help us to love one another.

Brother Sun and Sister Moon

We hear your tune

Open my eyes to see peace and justice

No one is left out

So much in love with all that I survey

Love awake our hearts

The Sacred Feminine and
Sacred Masculine know every orientation

Loves always was and always will be

This painting captures just a few of the people who had the courage to love, who worked for peace, who fought for justice, who battled for equality, who built models for living and who moved beyond stereotypes. They are:

St. Scholastica and St. Benedict
Gertrude Stein and Alice B. Toklas
St. Francis and St. Clare
Mothers and Children
Bishop Cosmas and Damien
Jesus and John the Beloved
K.D. Lang and Sandra Bernhard

Their message, their work, and their dreams were about all humanity being treated with dignity.

Many people have gone before us – holy men and women who have lighted the way for us. They were wise women and men employing the courage to stand up for justice and peace, the work for equality, the offer of hope and did not give up. They were prophets, mystics and martyrs:

Gandhi, Rumi, Hafiz, Hildegard of Bingen, Julian of Norwich, Lao Tzu, Anne Frank, Rabbi Heschel, Martin Luther King, The Dalai Lama, Mohammad, Chief Joseph, Jesus, Mary Magdalene, Buddha, Ita Ford, Dorothy Kazel, Maura Clarke, Jean Donovan, Mother Mary Rose, Mary McLeod Bethune, Pope John XXIII, Pope Francis, Stephen Biko, Harvey Milk, Eleanor Roosevelt and Abigail Scott Duniway.

These people held out the truth, respected all of humanity, worked with purpose, overcame many obstacles and followed their heart.

PRAYERS AND POEMS TO:
THE HISTORY

PRAYER TO COSMAS AND DAMIEN

Oh glorious martyrs, you gave your lives for the love of God and benefitting humanity and crowning your martyrdom with an open and loyal profession of your faith. You taught us to love God and to love all of humanity, professing always, without fear, love.

BROTHER SUN AND SISTER MOON

Brother Sun and Sister Moon, where are you
I rarely hear your tune
Distracted with fear
Brother Wind and Sister Air
Open my eyes to see pure and fair
I am a human being, I am a part
I feel His love in my heart.
Brother Sun and Sister Moon
Now I can see you
I can hear your tune.
So much in love
With what I can see.
    St. Francis

DO YOU NEED GOD

I realize I don't need God; I've already got one – women.
I realize I don't need God; I've already got one – men.

DAVID MOURNS JOHATHAN

O Jonathan, in your death I am stricken,
I am desolate for you, Jonathan, my brother.
Very dear to me you were,
Your love to me more wonderful
than the love of a woman.
    2 Samuel

CONVERSATION BETWEEN DAVID AND JOHATHAN

Whatever you want me to do, I'll do it for you
Then they kissed each other and wept together – but David wept the most.
Go in peace, for we have sworn friendship with each other in the name of the Lord, saying, 'The Lord is witness between you and me,
    and between your descendants and my descendants for ever."
    1 Samuel

PRAYER TO ST SCHOLASTICA

O God, to show us where innocence leads, you made the soul of your Scholastica soar to heaven like a dove in flight. Grant through her merits and her prayers that we may so live in innocence as to attain to joys everlasting.

PRAYER TO ST BENEDICT

Admirable Saint and Doctor of Humility,
    you practiced what you taught, assiduously praying for us.
Guard our hearts, minds, souls and bodies.
Practicing what you preached, you founded the monastic tradition.
Glorious St. Benedict, sublime model of virtue,
    I implore you in your loving kindness to all people.
May your blessing be with us always.

GOD'S ADMIRATION

God's admiration for us is infinitely greater than anything we can conjure up for Him (or Her).
    St. Francis of Assisi

TO ALL WHO CAME BEFORE

    To all those who came before
    To all those who came who do more
    Do more to open the doors to life
    Honoring the both/and of our nature
    Offering the possibility of wholeness, modeling wholeness.
    We give thanks.
        Annie Doyle

Chapter 6

THE COSMIC UNION

COSMIC UNION

(as seen on painting)

Women and men shine light on all

Together

One

Union

Moon and sun

Universally connected

We care for the universe

Hand in hand

Women and men

Stars of the universe

The universe of the

Sacred feminine and masculine

Inherently connected

Both/and

We are inherently connected. We are connected to the first cell and continue the journey through billions of years as co-creators, continuing the creation story. Whether it is micro or macro, known or unknown, seen or unseen; we are a part of it all.

The merge of the Sacred Feminine and Sacred Masculine is about embracing our whole self, connecting to others from wholeness and working in the world to end any form of oppression based on racism, sexism, homophobia, adultism or classism. It is also about connecting to all of creation including the vast universe.

This painting represents the sacred union bringing together everything in the world and outside the world.

Prayers and Poems to: Cosmic Union

The Universe as Brother and Sister

The universe is our sister and brother, we love her cosmic grace, we know that he loves us, we admire her strength and together their beauty delights us.
James Galluzzo

The Universe Garden

> The air smells good today
> straight from the mysteries
> within
> the garden
> of the universe.
> *Rumi*

Culture and Cosmos

Evolutionary spirituality calls us to participate in the deeper processes at work in the unfolding of culture and cosmos.

Many of us…are waking up to a new dimension of life in God that points us not beyond time, but toward the future we need to create.
Gail Worcel

Harmony

We have a deep faith that if humans could come into harmony with the real universe, our troubled species would have its best chance to enjoy this jewel of a planet, unique in all the cosmos.
Joel Primack

The Universe is a Communion

The universe is a communion of subjects, not a collection of objects. And listen to this: The human is derivative. The planet is primary.
Thomas Berry

LIVING INSIDE OF YOU

All the principles of heaven and earth are living inside of you. Life itself is truth, and this will never change. Everything in heaven and earth breathes. Breath is the thread that ties creation together.
    Morihei Ueshiba

AFTER YEARS

Today, from a distance, I saw you walking away, and without a sound
the glittering face of a glacier slid into the sea.
An ancient oak fell in the Cumberlands, holding only a handful of leaves,
and an old woman scattering corn to her chickens looked up for an instant,
At the other side of the galaxy,
a star thirty-five times the size of our own sun exploded and vanished,
leaving a small green spot on the astronomer's retina as he stood on the great open dome of my heart with no one to tell.
    Ted Koser

COSMIC UNION ANEW

Out my window--
    the rain falls--
        raindrops creating concentric circles in the puddles.
Tall firs sway in the wind
    rustling feathers of tiny birds.
The air and earth are drenched with wetness
    brightened by the dazzling golden daffodils.
From stardust came
    the rain and birds,
        the fir trees and air,
            the earth and the daffodils,
                and me.
All things are in communion with each other--
    giving life,
        enriching life,
           bringing wholeness to my soul.
My soul emerged from stardust,
    Entwined with the sun and the moon,
        the stars and the planets.
I am part of the family of things*.
The Universe and I are partners moving together in the dance
    of things known and unknown,
        discovered and yet to be discovered.
Always in touch--
    holy intimacy--
        cosmic union.
    Susan Hammond

* Mary Oliver, Wild Geese

This book is the culmination of ten years of research and sketches of what the merger of the Sacred Feminine and Sacred Masculine would look like. I began the sketches for the paintings for this third book first. Then I realized it would be important to write books and do paintings for the Sacred Feminine and Sacred Masculine. This was necessary to set the stage for the merger of the two and provide the prologue for the final book.

So now comes the third and final book in this series, *The Merge: A Reemerging of the Sacred Feminine and Sacred Masculine.*

The book presents a oneness with ourselves, others, the world and the universe. It is about wholeness; it is that we are "all connected." It is an experience of non-dualism and universal connection. This book is about the binder of love and loving all that was, all that is and all that will be.

It is my hope that each reader of this book will experience what a new Eden could look like through the words, poems and paintings, and people will then embrace their wholeness, the cosmic union, the "at one with" of the Sacred Feminine and Sacred Masculine. It is about the sacred humanness of all people within each person.

May this series show the way for each person to embrace his or her full humanity and live life without settling for anything less than Everything.

> "THE MERGER OF THE SACRED MASCULINE AND SACRED FEMININE CULTIVATES LOVE. THIS HAPPENS WHEN WE ALLOW OUR TRUE AND WHOLE SELF TO EMERGE, WHEN WE ALLOW OURSELVES TO BE SEEN, HEARD AND KNOWN. WHEN WE HONOR THE SACRED CONNECTION, ONENESS GROWS THROUGH TRANSFORMATION, LOVING KINDNESS, RESPECT AND HONORING THE GIFT OF DIVERSITY."
>
> JAMES GALLUZZO

JAMES GALLUZO

JAMES GALLUZZO has been a spiritual director and guide for 25 years, working with individuals, teaching classes, and giving retreats. He is an artist, author, priest, teacher, administrator, diversity trainer, and spiritual director.

Fr. Galluzzo is the author of: A Spiritual Handbook: A Resource for Travelers and Guides on the Journey, The Spirituality of Mary Magdalene, Jesus as Liberator and the Gospel Values, Quotes and Reflection Questions for Journaling your Spiritual Journey, Spiritual Writing: Be the Author of Your Own Story, and Stop Whining, Choose Life.

He founded Allies: People to People, an organization that teaches a way of living and thinking that honors human liberation based on the Gospel values, and that works to end oppression of any kind: sexism, racism, classism, ageism, adultism, and homophobia.

Fr. Galluzzo is the director of the non-profit organization Diversity as Gift that works to honor all and teach about dignity from a spiritual perspective. He is also the director of the Urban Spirituality Center in Portland, Oregon.

He holds a BA degree from Gonzaga University, an MAT degree from Reed College, an Administrative Certificate from Lewis and Clark College, an MA degree in Theology from Catholic University of America, Mount Angel Seminary, and Portland State University.

Fr. Galluzzo leads workshops throughout the country on Conflict Resolution, Community Building, Diversity, Gospel Values, Spirituality, and Human Liberation.

ACKNOWLEDGEMENTS

In gratitude for help and guidance from:
Jan Kruger

Janet Beard

Annie Doyle

Peg Edera

Susan Hammond

Ruth Nickodemus

Sheree Tuppan

Maureen Schwerdtfeger

Book and Cover Design by Karen Gatens, Gatens Design

www.ingramcontent.com/pod-product-compliance
Lightning Source LLC
Chambersburg PA
CBHW042003150426
43194CB00002B/114